PHILEMON
LIVED IN
COLOSSAE

CHRISTINE A. CORNELL

Printed in the United States of America

ISBN:
Softcover: 978-1-969367-77-9
Hardback: 978-1-969367-78-6
eBook: 978-1-969367-79-3

For permission requests, visit and write to the publisher at:

Publisher Name/Author: Christine A. Cornell
Phone/Mobile: (616) 250-2757
Email: thechristinecornell@yahoo.com
Website: https://thechristinecornell.com

Chapter 1

Philemon lived in Colossae. He owned a vineyard. He had recently lost a servant of 15 years to illness and needed a replacement. Horus had been a faithful servant and Philemon felt the loss. His thought was to find someone in a desperate situation who would be grateful for a master with simple expectations. Philemon felt sure a man in debtors' prison would be such a man. He did not consider the resentment a man would feel at being owned. Philemon assumed his last house servant was happy to be out of debtors' prison and acted accordingly. The idea that the man was being submissive to avoid punishment had not crossed Philemon's mind. He made the trip to Myra because there was a debtors' prison there and it was closer to the slave ships. Strong men could be found there. His house servant had come from the docks. Horus had accompanied Philemon many times, loading and unloading barrels of wine. This time he had taken two younger servants from the vineyard to take the barrels to the market. Philemon made his sales and went to the Roman tax collector to make his payment.

All three of them went into the debtors' prison. Inside the prison Philemon spoke to the warden. "Bring out to me those who are strong and in good health. I am looking for a house servant."

"I have three men for you to choose from," said the warden. The men came out in loin clothes so Philemon could see how healthy and strong they were.

"The man in the middle looks the healthiest," said Philemon.

"Onesimus is his name," said the warden. "A fitting name for a servant, don't you think?"

"What is the price?" asked Philemon. "What are his debts?"

"His creditors will let him go for six years wages," said the warden. "His is an unusual case. He was an indentured servant, working to earn a ship of his own. The ship on which he was serving was destroyed at sea. He was the sole survivor. He was imprisoned by the court to pay off the remaining years of service and the price of the ship. He has been looked at as a possible gladiator more than once."

"What a dreadful waste that would have been," said Philemon. "Gladiators have no hope of freedom and little hope of survival."

"Do you eventually plan to release him then?" asked the warden.

"That is my plan. If the man wishes to leave after seven years, he is free to go. If he is content, he can stay as a bond servant as Horus did," said Philemon. "I will take Onesimus. Here is a tunic for him and an armband to identify him as mine."

One of the servants with Philemon walked up to Onesimus and placed a band on his wrist. He fastened it with a clip. Then the servant pushed the band up his arm past the elbow. Onesimus' arm was pinched and cut by the pressure, but Onesimus did not react. He walked out of the prison with Philemon and the other servants. Philemon paid close attention to Onesimus. He had the look of a man from the sea; accustomed to hard work with his face weathered by the sun and wind. There was a look in Onesimus' eyes Philemon did not like. It was between resentment and resignation. He hoped the look would soften after being out of prison for a while. "Tell me about yourself Onesimus," said Philemon, hoping to soften the atmosphere.

"As the warden told you," said Onesimus, "I worked as an indentured servant on a cargo ship. I had entered into an agreement to work for a ship of my own. I did not see myself as an indentured servant but according to the law, that is what I was. On one trip at sea there was a terrible storm before we could make it to the shore. The captain who I worked for was killed and the ship destroyed. I survived the storm and returned to port. I truly believed I was a free man, able to pick another ship to serve on. Since I returned and the captain did not, the owners charged me for the price of the lost ship. It was a price I could not pay so I was thrown into prison. It is true I was looked at as a gladiator for the colosseum of Rome. Serving you is far from the open sea which I love, but it is better than I had come to expect"

Those words were a relief to Philemon. Perhaps it was Onesimus hard life that was etched in his face and not resentment. It might be a boring life for him as a household servant, but it would be a reprieve from his life so far. Anything was better than the life of a gladiator. Gladiators were chosen because they were hardened criminals, not men of the sea. When they reached the vineyard, Onesimus was shown his quarters. He would sleep in a room in the main house so he could hear his master when he called. He would prepare and serve the master's meals. Onesimus said he had been a cook aboard ship, so he knew his way around the kitchen. As a personal servant, he would also accompany Philemon on his business trips.

One day Philemon went to Ephesus to conduct business, and he took Onesimus with him to assist him. He was obedient, but there was a harshness about Onesimus when he dealt with the other servants, which Philemon did not like. On this trip Philemon hoped to see an improvement in Onesimus treatment of merchants and their servants. He was polite and loaded and unloaded the wine as instructed. Perhaps he was trying to prove himself to the other servants from back home.

After business was complete, Philemon often went to the Halls of Tyrannus to listen to the debates of the day. He had heard debates between the schools of philosophy, stoicism and disciples of Plato. Their views of life were not satisfying to Philemon. He believed there was more to who he was than his intellect. He was a spiritual being with an eternal soul. The gods Philemon had grown up hearing about were not concerned with the needs of mortals except when it affected their world. Judging by the legends he was taught; the gods and goddesses were fickle and had the same struggles as mortals.

This trip was different. Philemon listened to a Jewish preacher named Paul. This man spoke of the one true God who was holy and all powerful. He explained that God was holy and all powerful and none of us were worthy to stand before Him. God had sent a messiah, his Son, to reconcile us with Himself. God, the Father, wanted a relationship with us, his creation. Jesus had made this possible by taking the penalty for our sins. He died on a Roman cross and proved he was the Son of God by rising from the dead. The gift of eternal life was for anyone who believed.

Philemon did not need to be told what sin was. He knew he could not live up to his own standards, let alone those of a holy God. In his heart, Philemon had lived unconcerned about the plight of the other merchants. He was a reasonable master if his personal comforts were taken care of. He paid his taxes because he had to and did not concern himself with the needs of others. His desire for wealth and power had often blinded him to what his pursuit was costing those around him. In the end those pursuits had left him feeling empty and his life without meaning. He had not considered where he would go when he died. Here was a message about God who had made a way for him to know. Through all the references to ancient prophesies and the Jewish law, Philemon understood his need for a savior. He accepted the gift of salvation paid for by Jesus Christ and began a new life that day. Philemon walked up to Epaphras, one of Paul's followers.

"Up until now I have lived a selfish life," said Philemon. "I am wealthy, but my wealth does not satisfy. From what I have heard today, I have come to see my need for a new life in Jesus. I know Jesus Christ has forgiven me and reconciled me to God."

"As proof of your commitment, are you prepared to be baptized?" asked Epaphras.

"I am," said Philemon.

They walked down to the water with other new converts and disciples. When the two men walked into the water Epaphras asked, "Do you give up your old way of life and commit to follow Jesus Christ?"

"I do," said Philemon

"I baptize you in the name of the Father, Son and Holy Spirit" Epaphras stated. After speaking these words over him, he dipped Philemon under the water.

Philemon had a sudden understanding of a new life within him. He had laid down his old self and was a new person. As he left the water and came to shore, a couple came to greet Philemon.

"Hello Apphia and Archippus," said Epaphras and embraced them both. "This couple is from our community."

"Yes, I recognize them from the village," said Philemon.

"We have been listening to Paul for some time," said Archippus. "We have been wanting to find a place in Colossae to share the message of forgiveness with the people there."

"I want to share the message of this new life as well," said Philemon. "I am willing to open my home for anyone to teach about Jesus. We need someone familiar with the whole message to teach."

"I plan to travel with Paul where the Lord leads him," said Epaphras. "I will speak with Paul and explain your offer."

The four of them went together to speak to Paul. Paul agreed to part with Epaphras help for as long as Paul remained in Ephesus, for the sake of spreading the Gospel to Colossae. Paul continued to lecture in the Halls of Tyrannus. He continued to present the truth of man's sinful nature. He proclaimed the death and resurrection of Jesus Christ, the Son of God. He preached of the need to turn away from sin and be brought near to God. Many people of the area came to believe. There were signs of the presence of God being with Paul. The witness of the power of God was so great, even Paul's apron and handkerchief brought healing to those who touched them. As a show of repentance, people brought scrolls on divination and the occult to the disciples to be burned. The scrolls were worth 50,000 drachmas in total.

Back in Colossae, the believers shared the bread and the wine of the Lord's Supper, at Philemon's home. Onesimus waited at tables distributing the bread and the wine. He worked in the kitchen baking bread. When he was not in the kitchen, he would hear the hymns and songs. He heard Epaphras teach but he did not believe it. The idea of there being one true God intrigued him. It made sense. But he had given up on religion and did not think the gods cared about the lives of men. He saw the people embracing each other as they passed the loaves and wine. But Onesimus could not understand what it all meant. All he could think of was the freedom of the sea. Everything here was so predictable, so monotonous. There was no challenge with cooking and cleaning every day. He had tried to relate to the servants who served in the vineyard. They had been farming hands all their lives and had no dreams or at least did not share them. They appeared to be content. Onesimus had always wanted more and felt he could do better on his own.

Philemon chose Onesimus to escort his wine to Myra and to sell it. He would work as a merchant for his master. He was instructed to sell the wine and to bring back household supplies and pay the taxes. Philemon was called away to Ephesus to meet with the disciples there. There had been a riot in Ephesus and Paul had been asked to leave the area for his own safety. Paul wanted to say goodbye and give final instructions to the disciples. Philemon traveled to Ephesus with Apphia and Archippus and met Epaphras outside the city. Paul had called the disciples together to say he was going to Macedonia and Greece to share the message there.

Onesimus made a short trip to Myra. He was a salesman by nature and found it easy to sell his master's wine. He paid the taxes so he would draw less attention to himself when he left. With some of the remaining money he bought more suitable clothes for himself. He paid someone to remove the band from his arm. He went to the harbor to find a ship he could join. There was a crew mending the nets. At first Onesimus was afraid to approach. "What if they already knew I am a runaway," he thought. "What kind of ship do you sail," he asked. "I am looking to join a crew."

"We are a prison ship," said one of the men. "We escort prisoners to Rome, and we move cargo for our owner."

Onesimus shuddered at the word prisoner. If he was found out he could become one of the galley slaves or be executed by the guards for being an escaped slave. "I can work for my passage to the next port. If I perform to your satisfaction, I would like to stay on your ship. If not, I can find another ship to join where you deliver the prisoners," said Onesimus.

The men studied Onesimus closely. He appeared nervous as if he was hiding something. Some of them were apprehensive about taking a stranger on board. The captain, the one who had been answering Onesimus, spoke to his men in private. After some discussion the captain finally said, "I can handle this man if he becomes a problem."

He came back to Onesimus. "You look like a strong man," said the captain. "I believe you could handle the rudder, and you are forceful enough to command the rowers. You are hired. We sail in two days. You can bunk in the hold of the ship if you have nowhere to sleep in the city,"

"That will be fine," said Onesimus. "I can sleep anywhere. "What would you like me to do before we sail?"

"We are checking the nets for damage. We sometimes need them for fishing," said the captain. "You can take a seat over here next of Alexander." The man gave Onesimus a spool of twine and a shuttle. He began to wrap twine around the sections of the torn net. It was tedious work, but Onesimus was fine with it because he was free. When they all finished, it was sunset.

"You have earned a meal and a bed for the night," said the captain. "Come over by the fire and have some fish with us. My name is Philip, and these are my shipmates; Alexander who you have met, Simon, Demas and Aeneas."

"When do we sail?" asked Onesimus.

Captain Philip smiled at him. "You appear to be in a hurry to leave this harbor. We will be leaving for the next port as soon as we receive our cargo tomorrow."

Onesimus did not say anything more. He realized he had sounded too eager. He could not go back to his master. He had sold the pack mules and had no way back to the vineyard. He was committed now and would sail with these men.

The next day the men loaded cargo all day so it would mean another day in port. Onesimus knew Philemon would have been notified by now of his failure to return. The work on board the ship was harder than delivering wine or tending to the members of the household. Onesimus thought back to the strange ritual of sharing bread and wine. Instead of each person eating his own loaf and keeping his own wine skin, they shared both. Epaphras had explained that Jesus had started the ceremony the night before he was crucified by the Romans. Onesimus did not understand how the death of a man should start a religion.

The next morning it became clear what he was to do for the rest of the voyage. He would assist Alexander in commanding the rowers in the galley. Ordering slaves made Onesimus uncomfortable. If he was found out, he could be made a galley slave. He hated barking orders at the slaves. And he worried whether he would be listened to or challenged. Onesimus had to listen carefully to the rowing instructions of Captain Philip. Then he would give orders to the prisoners on the starboard side of the ship to row harder or less so accordingly.

At this time, Epaphras received a message that Paul wanted to see him. There had been a riot in Ephesus and Paul had been asked not to return for his own safety. Those believers who had heard Paul in the Hall of Tyrannous before were told about the riot, including Epaphras. These disciples of Paul went to see him outside the city. When they were together, they pleaded with Paul not to preach to the people in Ephesus. Paul requested that Epaphras go to Antioch to check on his ministry there. He wanted to know if they were continuing in faithfulness and giving as they had during the famine. Paul also was concerned about the ministry of Barnabas. Epaphras had to return to Colossae to explain Paul's request and to say goodbye to the house church there.

When Epaphras returned to Colossae, he went to speak with Philemon about his plans to leave. When the two men met, Philemon was preparing for a trip to Myra to find his missing servant and to purchase the goods for his household. He made plans to find out where Onesimus had gone and what happened to the wine. Philemon still could not understand the resentment of being owned.

"What would you do if you were in my place?" Philemon asked Epaphras.

"I would report Onesimus to the authorities," said Epaphras. "Explain you are not seeking death for him. I know that is within your rights. Tell them you are looking for his safe return to his duties. It is less likely your servant will be harmed when he is found.

"I am angry with Onesimus, but I don't want him harmed," said Philemon. "Perhaps I gave him an assignment he was not prepared for."

"Do you know what may have tempted him to leave?" he asked.

"All I know is what the other servants have said," answered Philemon. "He longed to be back at sea. When he spoke to the other servants about his life, that is what he talked about. I had planned to offer Onesimus his freedom after six years. Now I must consider the money he has taken. Why couldn't he have waited until his time was up?"

"I understand your anger about the missing money and the broken trust," said Epaphras. "Remember how much Christ has forgiven you. Onesimus does not know the freedom we have found in Christ. He believes life at sea is freedom.

"I am going to Myra tomorrow," said Philemon. "I will be traveling with two young servants."

"I would like to go with you instead," said Epaphras. "On the trip I can explain my future trip to Antioch."

"I am sorry to see you go," said Philemon. "I have been so concerned with my problem; I did not even ask about what happened in Ephesus."

"Paul stayed out of the city and the magistrate settled down the protest," said Epaphras. "Paul has felt led to leave the area. He has asked me to check on the ministry in Antioch and to obtain help from the brothers and sisters there. Apphia and Archippus are trained in the gospel and are well prepared to take my place."

"I know they are gifted teachers," said Philemon. "I wish you could stay and help sort out what to do. You have been my mentor since the beginning."

The next morning the two men started traveling together. Philemon thought about how he was going to approach the warden at the debtor's prison. He wasn't even sure it was the right place to start. He was the only one Philemon could think of who knew Onesimus by sight. Perhaps he would know where Onesimus would go. When they reached Myra, they parted. Philemon approached the prison to speak to the warden.

"I am Turabian," he said. "I have spoken to you before Master Philemon. Have you returned to purchase another slave?"

"Thank you, no," said Philemon. "I am hoping you can help me with another problem. My servant Onesimus is missing. I understand he is originally from this area. I wonder if you know where he might go?"

"I think I remember the man," said Turabian. "He was a man of the sea and survived a shipwreck. If he is a run-away, I would think he might attempt to get hired on another ship."

"Thank you for your help," said Philemon. "I will look for him at the harbor."

Philemon left the prison and headed for the harbor. Onesimus knew the city well. He could be hiding anywhere. He hoped Onesimus would return to what he was familiar with. He approached the first group of sailors he came to. The men were gathered, mending their nets.

"My name is Philemon, and I own a vineyard in Colossae," he said. "I am looking for a runaway slave named Onesimus. Have you seen anyone seeking to be hired."

The group of men looked at each other then continued working. Finally, the oldest sailor answered.

"I spoke to a captain of a prison ship who hired a man to command the rowers. His men were suspicious, but Captain Philip assured his crew, since he was able to handle a galley full of slaves, he could certainly handle one runaway. The crew decided to take advantage of the free labor before turning the man in. They left fully loaded a few days ago with slaves and cargo for Jerusalem.

"Then I will never recover him!" exclaimed Philemon.

"Don't give up hope, Master Philemon," said the sailor. "When he returns, I will tell the captain that Onesimus is your slave. After captain Philip gets done with Onesimus he will be glad to return to you."

"I guess all I can do is hope Captain Philip is a fair man, and my will return my slave," said Philemon. "Please ask him to be returned to the warden, Turabian, so I can retrieve him when I am able." Philemon turned to leave. His trip had not been a total waste. At least he knew where Onesimus was. He still had hope that Onesimus would return safely.

Philemon and Epaphras met on the road back to Colossae. Philemon began to explain what he had found out about Onesimus.

"I spoke with the warden at the debtor's prison," said Philemon. "He directed me to the docks. A fisherman told me of a man who joined crew of a slave ship. The ship departed for Jerusalem about the time Onesimus went missing. The fisherman promised to inform the captain of his new hire's identity. I asked that he be returned to the debtor's prison."

"I will continue to pray for his safe return," said Epaphras. "I am sure you will find a competent slave among the workers in your vineyard, to manage your household."

"Yes," said Philemon. "I have found two brothers who are new believers. I believe they will be faithful. They are eager to assist with the Lord's supper."

"I am glad the message is reaching the servants," said Epaphras. "I baptized many new believers who came to hear the good news of freedom in Christ. I will have to leave you here to continue my journey to Antioch." The two men embraced not knowing when they would see each other again.

The believers continued to meet on Sunday to break bread and for prayer. The brother servants baked the bread the day before. Archippus preached reconciliation to God through Christ. Apphia and Archippus assisted in answering questions and praying with new believers. This routine went on, week after week. The two servants living with Philemon, Marcus and Alpheus, accompanied him on his merchant trips, which he insisted on doing himself. Despite the submission and faithfulness of the brothers, Philemon did not trust them to go alone with his goods.

One day the church received word that Paul had returned to Assos to meet with the elders of Ephesus, and the leaders at Colossae were invited to join them. Archippus and Philemon traveled together. He could tell that the joy and hope Philemon had expressed in the beginning of his faith was decreasing. Archippus felt sure it had something to do with the loss of his servant and the departure of Epaphras. Archippus had not established the same kind of relationship as Philemon had with Epaphras. Archippus had preached the call of the Holy Spirit on a believer's life and that the spirit moved differently in each of them. He had tried to explain the need for trust and obedience when doors open. Philemon had nodded in agreement with the message but there was still sadness in his face. Archippus did not know what more to say. So, he prayed as they walked together.

When they got to the town of Assos, Paul was waiting. He explained that he was led to return to Jerusalem to present the gospel to his fellow Jews. He was surrounded by his future traveling companions. After they pleaded with Paul for an hour not to go, Paul addressed the elders. He said:

"You know how I lived the whole time I was with you, from the first day I came into the province of Asia. I served the Lord with great humility and with tears and in the midst of severe testing by the plots of my Jewish opponents. You know that I have not hesitated to preach anything that would be helpful to you but have taught you publicly and from house to house. I have declared to both Jews and Greeks that they must turn to God in repentance and have faith in our Lord Jesus. And now, compelled by the Spirit, I am going to Jerusalem, not knowing what will happen to me there. I only know that in every city the Holy

Spirit warns me that prison and hardships are facing me. However, I consider my life worth nothing to me; my only aim is to finish the race and complete the task the Lord Jesus has given me--the task of testifying to the good news of God's grace. "Now I know that none of you among whom I have gone about preaching the kingdom will ever see me again. Therefore, I declare to you today that I am innocent of the blood of any of you. For I have not hesitated to proclaim to you the whole will of God. Keep watch over yourselves and all the flock of which the Holy Spirit has made you overseers. Be shepherds of the church of God, which he bought with his own blood. I know that after I leave, savage wolves will come in among you and will not spare the flock. Even from your own number men will arise and distort the truth to draw away disciples after them. So be on your guard! Remember that for three years I never stopped warning each of you night and day with tears. "Now I commit you to God and to the word of his grace, which can build you up and give you an inheritance among all those who are sanctified. I have not coveted anyone's silver or gold or clothing. You yourselves know that these hands of mine have supplied my own needs and the needs of my companions. In everything I did, I showed you that by this kind of hard work we must help the weak, remembering the words the Lord Jesus himself said: 'It is more blessed to give than to receive.' " When Paul had finished speaking, he knelt down with all of them and prayed. They all wept as they embraced him and kissed him.[1]

---

[1]   *Acts 20:18-37*

Chapter 2

A few weeks later the slave ship returned to Myra with Onesimus still on board. The whole trip was stressful. Onesimus worried the whole trip that the galley slaves would recognize him. None of them said anything. Onesimus was conscious of the mark left on his arm by the band. He was sure his shipmates knew. They had asked him about his earlier life. Onesimus had explained he had been an indentured servant on board a ship which was lost at sea with him the only survivor. It was true, but he told only part of the story. In truth, Onesimus deserved to be one of the galley slaves. After hours of loading cargo from the area, Captain Philip and his crew walked to an inn near the docks, while the galley slaves remained chained to their station. Onesimus remained with the prisoners.

The old fisherman who had spoken to Philemon was at the inn also. He called Captain Phillip to sit with him. "You hired a new man I see," said the fisherman. "Where does he come from?"

"He told me he comes from this city. He grew up here," stated Captain Philip. "He had always wanted to go to sea. He made himself a servant to earn a ship of his own. Before he could work off the cost of the ship, it was lost at sea. He was looking for another ship to be hired on when he came to mine."

"That is strange," said the fisherman. "A gentleman was looking for a runaway slave who knew the port well. I was sure your new mate was a runaway." Captain Philip thought for a moment of the mark on Onesimus' arm and his eagerness to be at sea. He said nothing.

The fisherman continued, "The gentleman's name was Philemon. He owns a vineyard in Colossae. He was a peaceful man and did not want the slave harmed, just returned."

"Where was he to be returned?" Captain Philip asked. "Colossae is a long way from port."

Master Philemon wanted him returned here to the debtors' prison where he had bought him," said the fisherman.

"But as you say, the stories do not match," said Captain Philip. "I am glad you told me. I would not want to be going against the Roman authorities."

Before going to his room that night, Captain Philip came back to the ship to see Onesimus. He called Onesimus up from the galley to meet with him. "I have received information about your past life," he said. "You are a slave of Master Philemon of Colossae. He came to the docks looking for you."

Onesimus was startled and did not know what to say.

"Is it true?" asked Captain Philip.

"Yes, it is," Onesimus answered reluctantly.

"I have a dilemma," said Captain Philip. "You are a fugitive aboard my ship I work for the Roman authorities in managing and transporting slaves. It would pain me to lose you but if you're discovered, I would have to turn you over."

"But how can I go back now?!" exclaimed Onesimus. "My master can have me killed."

"I don't think he would do that," said Captain Philip calmly. "He wants his investment back. The way I see it, you can go back to debtor's prison until Master Philemon retrieves you, or you can take your chances with me and continue commanding the rowers onboard my ship."

"I need time to consider this," said Onesimus. "Please don't call the authorities yet."

"I won't if you don't bolt on me. "If you do, I will report you," Captain Philip said.

"I understand," said Onesimus, "either way I am no longer a free man."

"You never were free," said Captain Philip said with a smile. "Here is a leather band to cover the scar on your arm. My other men wear them, so it won't be suspicious."

Onesimus spent the night thinking about his situation. He felt as trapped now as he did with Philemon. Only this situation was worse. If he bolted now, he could end up in prison charged as a criminal and chosen as a gladiator or executed outright. If another man purchased him from prison before Philemon could reach him, his working conditions could be unbearable. He determined he would continue to manage the galley slaves as if he were a free man. He would maintain order and make himself indispensable to the captain and crew. Maybe they would still treat him as a free man.

Onesimus greeted the crew the next morning, tired but determined. Captain Philip ordered Onesimus to his position inside the ship. Onesimus went down to the galley of the ship with the galley slaves. These men also came from the debtor's prison. They were to be traded for a new set of rowers when the ship reached the next port. Galley slaves were highly valued as strong men. There was a need for such men wherever they were going. It was the strength Onesimus gained as a seaman that made him valuable to Philemon. The thought of his place at the vineyard did not seem so terrible. Maybe if he had stayed, he would have grown to accept his place in the household.

The men were each shackled to his place at the oars, because there was no way of knowing how desperate these men were. Some were true criminals who lived off from others or had outright stolen from merchants. Others had simply failed to please their master and were being replaced. All had a look of despair and hopelessness in their eyes. They could not imagine a master like Philemon who treated Onesimus well, like part of the family. There was no way Onesimus could offer hope to these men without giving himself away.

After the ship was underway for a time, Captain Philip came down to the galley to speak with Onesimus. He brought Onesimus up on deck and left Alexander in charge.

"Put your arm band on so you look like one of us," said Captain Philip. "You will wear this tunic also, so the slaves will relate to you better. To help the men row together, you will beat the drum instead of calling out. Leave that to Alexander."

"Yes captain," said Onesimus. "Then do all the men know?"

"Yes, I discussed it with them last night," said Captain Philip. "They were not surprised. They noticed the scar on your arm. You see, I told them we would have many ports to go to before returning to Myra. I wanted them all to have an eye on you, so you won't run or cause a mutiny with the galley slaves."

"But the other slaves can't know!" Onesimus exclaimed. "If they do, they may not obey me!"

"That is why I put Alexander in charge," said Captain Philip.

"I understand," was all Onesimus said. He was now Captain Philip's slave. He hoped he would make it back to Myra to turn himself in

The days at sea all seemed to blend. Onesimus lost track of time while he was in the galley. The days were broken up by visits to different ports. Every night in port, Onesimus slept in the hold of the ship. There was no point in going ashore. It was obvious to Onesimus that he did not belong at the inn.

The ship eventually made it back to Myra. When Onesimus approached the captain to turn himself in, the captain objected.

"You're too valuable to me now," said Captain Philip. "I don't want to leave you to waste away, waiting for your master to retrieve you. That could take months, and you would have no provisions while you wait after your money runs out.

"I was provided for in prison with help from my friends and relatives," said Onesimus.

"I do not have time to search for your relatives and friends," said Captain Philips. "We must load our next set of rowers and cargo."

"May I go ashore and look for my relatives this evening?" asked Onesimus.

"I cannot allow you to go alone, and I have no one to go with you. The crew is tired from the last voyage."

"But you promised I would have a choice next time we were in port!" exclaimed Onesimus.

Captain Philip just walked away and Onesimus returned to the cargo hold of the ship. Onesimus was trapped and now he knew it. With Philemon he could run his own kitchen and had some freedom. He was sent out on his own to sell Philemon's wine. And he had repaid that trust by leaving. Onesimus had another restless night.

The next morning was hard work because Onesimus had not rested well. He had never been allowed to give orders to the galley slaves. He could not ask one of them for help loading the cargo. It seemed to him, the rest of the crew did less and less labor with each harbor they came to. It was true at Myra as well. The other galley slaves were all loaded and chained to their station. Then Onesimus was finally able to take his seat at the drum. There was now a chain by the stool where he sat. Onesimus knew it was meant as a warning not to rebel or cause trouble or he would be chained too.

The days at sea seemed endless. The harbors they stopped at all looked the same viewed from the ship. This went on for two years with the crew wintering in different ports each year. They were due to winter in Myra this time around. Onesimus was in hopes he could finally persuade Captain Philips to let him speak with his family and return to the prison to be found by Philemon.

Chapter 3

The ship's next port was Sidon. Here captain Philip would trade for a new set of galley slaves. He asked Onesimus to come to shore as there was no one to stay with him. Onesimus at first welcomed the chance to live like a free man for a day. Then he worried something would happen and the captain would betray him. While Captain Philip was looking over the slaves, Onesimus went for a walk. At that time Epaphras was speaking to Paul and his companions, Timothy, Luke and Aristarchus. Onesimus recognized Epaphras right away. He hoped he would not be recognized.

"I am happy that I found you!" exclaimed Epaphras said to Paul. "I have gifts here from the church in Antioch. They sent me to see your needs were taken care of on your trip to Rome. I was hoping to join you on your journey."

"Welcome brother," said Paul. "Thank you for your gifts. I am considered a prisoner of Rome, so I have no right to ask for you. But if you can buy passage with us, you are welcome too. The man you need to speak to is somewhere nearby.

This must be the man who preached to Philemon in Ephesus, thought Onesimus. *I would like to understand why Paul is so willing to go to Rome to defend his message.*

Epaphras saw Onesimus listening and recognized him. He did not want to scare Onesimus away. He had to tell the truth, however. "Hello Onesimus, what brings you to Sidon?" he asked.

"Hello," said Onesimus. "You are the man who taught in Philemon's home. I am serving onboard a ship docked here."

Epaphras said, "Philemon has been looking for you, He was angry when you left him. He had hoped you would be returned to the debtor's prison where he could retrieve you."

Onesimus hesitated for a moment and then he said. "I would gladly return to Philemon if you could ensure my safety. I am no freer on my ship I serve on than in Philemon's home."

"It is good to hear you say you wish to return peacefully," said Epaphras.

Nearby Captain Philip and a soldier were listening. Captain Philip became angry. "I put my neck out to give that man a place on my crew," he muttered. "And this is the thanks I get."

"The fugitive is from your ship then?" asked the soldier.

"Yes, he is," said Captain Philip.

"Don't trouble yourself any longer," said the soldier. "I am Julius, a Centurion of the Imperial Regiment and I have the authority to arrest this man on the spot. We will eventually reach Myra. By then I will know what to do with him."

"I hope you make him a galley slave," said Captain Philip. "That is what he deserves." As Julius walked towards the group conversing together, the captain walked toward his ship. He was angry about losing free labor and felt betrayed. But he comforted himself with the thought of Onesimus being chained to the oars on his next ship.

As Julius approached Onesimus was asking Paul a question. "I do not understand your message. Which of the gods do you serve?"

I serve the one true God, the God of my ancestors. God sent his son in the person of Jesus Christ to pay the penalty for sin by dying on a Roman cross. He proved his power over sin and death by rising from the dead."

"How does the death of one man pay for all my failures and transgressions?" asked Onesimus

"Jesus was human and yet lived without sin. His death is the only payment for our sins. This Jesus is the one promised by the Law and the prophets of the Jews. I am a Jew and at one time, a persecutor of the church of Jesus Christ. I thought I was protecting the traditions of our fathers. I was on my way to Damascus to hunt down those who followed Jesus and to silence them. On my way to Damascus, I was halted by a light and a voice from heaven which said, 'Saul, Saul why do you persecute me.?!'"

"'Who are you, Lord?' I asked."

"'I am Jesus, who you are persecuting,' he replied. 'Now get up and go into the city and you will be told what you must do." I was blinded by the brilliant light and had to be led to the city by those traveling with me. They heard thunder but not the voice I heard. I stayed where I was led for three days.

"A man was sent to restore my sight, and he told me, 'the God of our ancestors has chosen you to know his will and to see the righteous one and to hear words from his mouth. You are my chosen instrument to proclaim my name to the Gentiles and their kings and to the people of Israel. Come and be filled with the Holy Spirit.'"

"When I received the Holy Spirit, the plan of God was revealed to me with the help of my knowledge of the scriptures. It was clear to me that the Christ must come and die to pay for sin and defeat sin, which the law could never do."

At this point Julius walked up to Epaphras and Onesimus. He called over another soldier. The other soldier grabbed Onesimus' arms and tied them behind his back. As Onesimus was being led away, he cried out. "I was going to turn myself in!"

"I don't know if you would or not," Julius said. "I'm not sure your captain would have let you go. He had free labor after all."

Epaphras was alarmed by Onesimus' arrest. He did not want him punished for fleeing, just returned to Philemon. Epaphras also wanted to obtain passage with Paul. The centurion had acted favorably with Paul in allowing him to seek help from his friends in Antioch. He hoped Julius would act favorably with him as well. He was in no position to seek favor with the centurion for someone else until he had obtained it for himself.

"I understand you are responsible for Paul's passage to Rome," said Epaphras.

"He is a Roman citizen, he is in my custody, and his safety is my responsibility," said Julius.

"I wish to accompany Paul to Rome and assist him," said Epaphras. "Do I have your permission to sail with you?"

"Passage for Paul has been bought by the Roman government," said Julius. "You will have to purchase your own."

"I have the means to do so," said Epaphras. "I also have supplies for our journey from his friends in Antioch."

Julius and Epaphras went in search of the captain. Julius found him watching the cargo loaded. He was giving orders to his men when they approached.

"Captain," said Julius. "This man is seeking passage on your ship with Paul. Can you accommodate him?"

"We are primarily a cargo ship," said the captain. "Paul and his companions have all the passenger quarters taken. "We have space in the cargo hold and a spare mat to sleep on."

"Thank you, captain," said Epaphras. "I am sure that will be sufficient for me. I am one of Paul's disciples and have been looking for him since I heard he was travelling to Rome. I have brought provisions for Paul from friends in Antioch. I can pay for my passage."

"Since you have brought your own provisions, payment will not be necessary," said the captain.

"We are only on this ship until we reach the next port, which is Myra," said Julius. "I will be looking for a different ship.

"We are heading to our home port in Adramyttium for the winter," said the captain. "Perhaps the next ship will have better accommodations for you and your friends."

"I have a favor to ask you as well," said Julius. "I have a prisoner who is a runaway slave. Can you use him in your galley?"

"Yes, we can," said the captain. "We are in need of a galley slave."

"I am aware Onesimus belongs to a man in Colossae, Epaphras," said Julius. "This is the best I could do for the slave. I don't know if I will have the opportunity to return him. My primary responsibility is to Paul and his companions."

"I understand your position," said Epaphras. "They are your prisoners because Paul appealed to Caesar and so is Onesimus since he is a runaway slave. Onesimus is a strong man. He can handle the job." Epaphras prayed no harm would come to Onesimus before he was returned to his master.

Epaphras boarded the ship and met up with Paul and his companions. He gave Paul the donations from the church in Antioch. Then he was taken to the cargo hold. There was some light from the entryway, which was the only source of light. He dropped his bedroll there and went to the passenger hold near the front of the ship as it left the harbor. Between the cargo hold and the passenger hold were the galley slaves. These men were not chained in place as slaves on Captain Philip's ship. They were controlled just by having Roman soldiers on board. Onesimus was at the front of the row. It was hard labor. Onesimus had not worked this hard since his early days on his first ship. He was a young man then, only sixteen. He could hoist the sail and man the ropes with any seasoned sailor. Now he was older and worn out by life. Life with Philemon did not seem so hard. If being a slave was his destiny, Philemon was a good master to have. As Onesimus rowed to the beat of the drum, his mind went to Paul's story. He still could not believe or understand the God Paul spoke of.

Chapter 4

The next port they reached was Myra. Julius was informed by the captain the ship would only be ashore until morning. Julius went with the soldiers to another ship bound for Italy. He obtained passage for the soldiers and Paul's company, then he hurried to the galley to get Onesimus. He was determined to check out Onesimus' story and attempt to get him back to his master. Julius left another soldier in charge and told the others not to go ashore until he returned. Then Julius and Onesimus headed away from the docks and to the debtor's prison.

"May I speak with the warden?" asked Julius.

"I am the warden. My name is Turabian," said the man at the door. "How may I help you, sir? Are you looking for a servant? I have many young men."

"No, I am not interested in purchasing a slave," said Julius. "I have a fugitive slave here who belongs to Master Philemon. Do you remember this man?"

Onesimus stepped forward and looked at Turabian. "Yes, I do remember you," answered Turabian. 'It has been over three years since I sold you. Philemon still comes here to look for you"

"So, he will come to retrieve me!" exclaimed Onesimus.

"It isn't that simple," said Turabian. "I must house you here and you have no provisions. I get no money for you when Philemon comes unless he provides a reward."

"Do I have time to contact my relatives in town and let them know I am here?" asked Onesimus.

"Only if they are nearby," said Julius.

"I can think of one relation who helped me when I was here before," said Onesimus.

"That would be sufficient for your provision," said Turabian.

"We must go quickly," said Julius. "We need to be back to the ship tonight." The two men walked about five blocks. When Onesimus knocked on the door a man answered who Onesimus did not recognize.

"I am looking for Arthur," said Onesimus. "He lived here with his family before you."

The man at the door was startled at the sight of a Roman soldier. "Arthur sold this to me and moved to the edge of town."

"We have no time to go looking any further," said Julius. "I must return to the ship to oversee the transfer of goods and prisoners."

"What will you do with me?" asked Onesimus.

"I will think of what to do with you on the way back to the ship," said Julius.

"Yes sir," said Onesimus. The two men walked in silence back to the ship.

"I will talk to the captain of the next ship concerning you tomorrow morning," said Julius. He escorted Onesimus to his station at the oars and went to the ship's passenger hold. Being a military man, Julius had to follow the law. Onesimus must remain a prisoner until he reaches Rome. Julius would plead for Onesimus' life with the prison in Rome.

Onesimus laid down on his bench to sleep. He felt totally defeated and exhausted. He knew he had no basis to plead for mercy. In Rome, he would be eligible for assignment as a gladiator. That was the same as a death sentence for all but the survivor. It was hard to say which was worse, starving in debtor's prison waiting for Philemon or fighting for his life in the Colosseum. That night he dreamed of fighting some of the men he had met on Captain Philip's ship. Then he dreamed of being behind the prison door, completely alone. He dreamed of walking back to Philemon's home. When he arrives at the house, Philemon will not see him. When morning came, he was in the galley again. He ate what was given to him, then followed the soldiers to the Alexandrian ship they were to sail on.

"I don't really need another slave at the oars. My crew takes charge of commanding the rowers," explained the captain. "To keep him occupied on the voyage, he could serve your men and the prisoners you are responsible for. Then my men could concentrate on their other duties

"That is an excellent solution," said Julius. "Onesimus is already acquainted with one of the passengers. He is also familiar with serving at the table."

"I would be happy to wait on Paul and his company as well as the soldiers," said Onesimus. *Finally, I will be able to ask about the God Paul serves*, he thought.

Onesimus was taken to where the food was stored. In the corner was a mat and a cloche for him to wrap up in at night. There were barley cakes and a barrel of bread without yeast. There were dates and raisin cakes and some olives and olive oil. The ship was well stocked for the voyage when they left the harbor.

The ship headed for Cnidus along the coast, but the wind took the ship off course and out to the island of Crete. The ship was forced to the south side known as Fair Haven. It was mid-October, and they had lost much time fighting the wind. Paul had spent much time in prayer and warned the crew against traveling further until spring. Julius did not listen to Paul's warning but agreed with the crew. Because it did not appear to be a safe harbor to winter in, they planned to spend the winter in Phoenix

When a gentle south wind began to blow, they saw their opportunity; so they weighed anchor and sailed along the shore of Crete. Before very long, a wind of hurricane force, called the Northeaster, swept down from the island. The ship was caught by the storm and could not head into the wind; so we gave way to it and were driven along. As we passed to the lee of a small island called Cauda, we were hardly able to make the lifeboat secure, so the men hoisted it aboard. Then they passed ropes under the ship itself to hold it together. Because they were afraid they would run aground on the sandbars of Syrtis, they lowered the sea anchor and let the ship be driven along. We took such a violent battering from the storm that the next day they began to throw the cargo overboard. On the third day, they threw the ship's tackle overboard with their own hands. When neither sun nor stars appeared for many days and the storm continued raging, we finally gave up all hope of being saved.

After they had gone a long time without food, Paul stood up before them and said: "Men, you should have taken my advice not to sail from Crete; then you would have spared yourselves this damage and loss. But now I urge you to keep up your courage, because not one of you will be lost; only the ship will be destroyed. Last night an angel of the God to whom I belong and whom I serve stood beside me and said, 'Do not be afraid, Paul. You must stand trial before Caesar; and God has graciously given you the lives of all who sail with you. So keep up your courage, men, for I have faith in God that it will happen just as he told me. Nevertheless, we must run aground on some island."

On the fourteenth night we were still being driven across the Adriatic Sea, when about midnight the sailors sensed they were approaching land. They took soundings and found that the water was a hundred and twenty feet deep. A short time later they took soundings again and found it was ninety feet deep. Fearing that we would be dashed against the rocks, they dropped four anchors from the stern and prayed for daylight. In an attempt to escape from the ship, the sailors let the lifeboat down into the sea, pretending they were going to lower some anchors from the bow. Then Paul said to the centurion and the soldiers, "Unless these men stay with the ship, you cannot be saved. So the soldiers cut the ropes that held the lifeboat and let it drift away.[2] Paul later urged them all to eat something and broke the bread and prayed a blessing over it as Epaphras had done at Philemon's house.

The next morning, they went ashore on the island of Malta. Once again Onesimus' life was endangered when the other soldiers wanted the kill all the prisoners to prevent them from escaping. Such a mass escape could cost a soldier his life. Julius did not let them do this because he valued Paul's courage and trusted him to stay with the soldiers. None of the galley slaves ran away for the same reason. He created so much confidence, the others followed Paul's leadership. Onesimus went to Epaphras as soon as everyone was safe ashore.

"Where does Paul's great faith come from?" asked Onesimus.

"Paul had a personal encounter with Jesus Christ, the risen Son of God," said Epaphras. "This is the one who he preaches. He can explain his story better himself."

At that time, Paul and some other men were gathering wood for a fire so everyone could dry off and get warm. Suddenly, a snake bit Paul on the arm. He shook it off and kept on working as if nothing had happened. The people of the island expected Paul to die because the snake was poisonous. When nothing happened, they concluded he was

---

[2]   Acts 27:13-32

one of the gods. Paul pleaded with the people not to worship him. He was only a servant of the one true God. Paul explained his experience with the risen Christ.

Paul and his company were welcomed by Publius, the official of the island. They stayed on his estate for three days. Onesimus continued working as a servant. Publius father was sick, and Paul placed his hands on him, and he was healed. The whole group wintered on the island for three months. Then the group boarded another Alexandrian ship bound for Italy. [3]

Onesimus listened to Paul's testimony of his encounter with Christ on the road to Damascus. That was when he explained his call to preach the good news to those who were not Jews like himself. The Christ came for everyone who would believe. Paul went on to explain Christ, the Messiah had been promised in scripture since before the giving of the law. Salvation was a gift paid for by the death of Christ. The resurrection proved to Paul that Jesus Christ was the one promised to defeat sin. He said that he was compelled to preach the gospel.

Julius continued to have Onesimus serve Paul and his companions as well as the other soldiers. He went to Epaphras to discuss what would happen once they reached Rome.

"Onesimus had adapted quite well to serving Paul. I believe he can be trusted to stay with you wherever you live in Rome. We should be able to convince the court to allow you to take responsibility for him," said Julius.

"I would be glad to do so. I am a servant of Paul's myself and plan to assist him in Rome for as long as he needs me," said Epaphras.

"That will be good," said Julius. "The regiment does not really have time to return slaves. I feel it would be a waste for him to end up a prisoner in Rome, or a galley slave, and never make it home to his master."

---

[3]   *Acts 28:1-10*

"I agree," said Epaphras. "As Philemon's friend, I can represent him and return Onesimus when the way is made for me to return to Colossae."

When the ship got to Rhegium, Paul was met by some of the followers in Rome. They explained that the Jews in Rome had not received any letter concerning his message. Three days later he called together the local Jewish leaders. When they had assembled, Paul said to them: "My brothers, although I have done nothing against our people or against the customs of our ancestors, I was arrested in Jerusalem and handed over to the Romans. They examined me and wanted to release me, because I was not guilty of any crime deserving death. The Jews objected, so I was compelled to make an appeal to Caesar. I certainly did not intend to bring any charge against my own people. For this reason I have asked you to see and talk with you. It is because of the hope of Israel that I am bound with this chain."

They replied, "We have not received any letters from Judea concerning you, and none of our people who have come from there has reported or said anything bad about you. But we want to hear what your views are, for we know that people everywhere are talking against this sect.

They arranged to meet Paul on a certain day and came in even larger numbers to the place where he was staying. He witnessed to them from morning till evening, explaining about the kingdom of God, and from the Law of Moses and from the Prophets he tried to persuade them about Jesus. Some were convinced by what he said, but others would not believe. They disagreed among themselves and began to leave after Paul had made this final statement:

"The Holy Spirit spoke the truth to our ancestors when he said through Isaiah the prophet:

'Go to this people and say, "You will be ever hearing but never understanding; you will be ever seeing but never perceiving." For this people's heart has become calloused, they hardly hear with their ears, and they have closed their eyes. Otherwise, they might see with their eyes, hear with their ears, understand with their hearts and turn, and I would heal them.[4]

---

[4]   *Acts 28:19-28*

Chapter 5

With the money Paul had received from Antioch and the believers in Rome, he rented a house. He was under house arrest while his case was brought before Caesar. Paul had many visits from the believers living in Rome. Tychicus had arrived with Paul and served as one of his scribes. He was from Ephesus and was planning to return to the believers there when Paul no longer needed him in Rome. Paul took a special interest in Onesimus and his dilemma. There were many injustices in the gentile communities which could benefit from the grace of Christ. One of them was slavery. Paul had preached the freedom in Christ to believers throughout Asia. He also believed he needed to explain the equality of all men before God. He also taught the obligation of members of a Christian household to live a life of submission and love. Within a community of believers, servants had an obligation to submit as well. Onesimus had met with misfortune in his life, but he still had an obligation to Philemon, the one who had purchased him for his debts. So, after Paul had addressed the freedom in Christ and the need for order in the believer's lives, he included the relationship between slave and master. Paul included these admonitions in his letters to Colossian and Ephesians.

When he had finished dictating his letters to the churches, he spoke to the group who were with them. He explained his thoughts concerning Onesimus.

"I know you once felt trapped in the life of a slave, Onesimus," said Paul. "Do you feel differently now that you have been set free from sin and made a brother in Christ?"

Onesimus thought for a moment. "I am at peace with my place in life now that I have found Christ," he said. "I have tried to serve you as well as I would Philemon. You and Epaphras saved me from a life as a galley slave."

"Please understand Onesimus," explained Paul. "The institution of slavery has a long history. Men have been lording it over other men for ages. I believe we as Christians should submit to the governing authorities. You should be returned to your master."

"I am willing to return to Philemon's house," said Onesimus. "I know the law. I am worried because it has been so long, and Philemon has every right to send me back to prison."

"I have met Philemon before. I will appeal to him for you. I will dictate the letter before you leave for Colossae with Tychicus," said Paul. "He will be my representative to the church since I cannot leave."

"I will take your message to the church in Colossae before we go to see Philemon," said Tychicus.

"I wish I was going too," said Epaphras. "I am not able to make the journey. When I am able, I must return to the Church in Antioch and explain how things are with Paul."

Paul dictated the following letter to his scribe:

Paul, a prisoner of Christ Jesus, and Timothy our brother,

To Philemon our dear friend and fellow worker—also to Apphia our sister and Archippus our fellow soldier—and to the church that meets in your home:

Grace and peace to you from God our father and the Lord Jesus Christ.

I always thank my God as I remember you in my prayers, because I hear about your love for all his holy people and your faith in the Lord Jesus. I pray that your partnership with us in the faith may be effective in deepening your understanding of every good thing we share for the sake of Christ. Your love has given me great joy and encouragement, because you, brother, have refreshed the hearts of the Lord's people.

Therefore, although in Christ I could be bold and order you to do what you ought to do, yet I prefer to appeal to you on the basis of love. It is as none other than Paul—an old man and now also a prisoner of Christ Jesus—that I appeal to you for my son Onesimus who became my son while I was in chains. Formerly he was useless to you, but now he has become useful both to you and to me.

I am sending him—who is my very heart-back to you. I would have liked to keep him with me so that he could take your place in helping me while I am in chains for the gospel. But I did not want to do anything without your consent, so that any favor you do would not seem forced but would be voluntary. Perhaps the reason he was separated from you for a little while was that you might have him back forever—no longer as a slave, but as a fellow man and as a brother in the Lord.

So if you consider me as a partner, welcome him as you would welcome me. If he has done you any wrong or owes you anything, charge it to me. I, Paul, am writing the with my own hand, I will pay it back—not to mention that you owe me your very self. I do wish, brother I may have some benefit from you in the Lord; refresh my heart in Christ. Confident of your obedience, I write to you knowing that you will do even more than I ask.

And one thing more: Prepare a guest room for me, because I hope to be restored to you in answer to your prayers. Epaphras, my fellow prisoner in Christ Jesus, sends you greetings. And so do Mark, Aristarchus, Demas and Luke, my fellow workers.

The grace of the Lord Jesus Christ be with your spirit.[5]

The following Sunday the brothers all shared the Lords Supper together. Onesimus assisted with the distribution of bread and wine. Paul prayed a blessing over the bread and then the wine.

He said: "For I received from the Lord what I also passed on to you: The Lord Jesus, on the night he was betrayed, took bread, and when he had given thanks, he broke it and said, "'This is my body, which was broken for you; do this in remembrance of me.' In the same way, after supper he took the cup saying, 'This cup is the new covenant in my blood; do this, whenever you drink it, in remembrance of me.' For whenever you eat this bread and drink this cup, you proclaim the Lord's death until he comes."[6]

For the first time Onesimus understood the meaning of the ritual. He understood Christ had died for him—had taken his place of punishment before God. He also understood the need to turn away from rebellion and toward a walk with Jesus Christ—to surrender to his lordship.

"Can you take me to the place where other believers are baptized?" asked Onesimus.

"There is a cistern behind the house where the disciples do their baptisms," answered Paul.

The believers who were meeting at Paul's house followed Onesimus out to the cistern. Epaphras asked him to express what he had come to believe

---

5   Philemon
6   1 Corinthians 11:23-26

"I believe Jesus Christ is the Son of God. I believe he suffered and died for me. I believe He is alive because of the miracles I have seen in his name. I believe Christ loves me because of the way I have been rescued from an empty life of slavery to a meaningful life of service to the kingdom. I admit I have lived a sinful life—living only for myself. I am changed because of Christ," Onesimus proclaimed.

"By your testimony my brother you have turned from your old life of rebellion and sin. You have turned from worshipping gods made by men to follow Jesus Christ," said Epaphras. "Therefore, I baptize you in the name of the Father, the Son and the Holy Spirit. United with Christ in his death and raised to new life." Epaphras laid him in the water and stood him to his feet.

Chapter 6

In the week that followed Tychicus and Onesimus prepared for their journey. The church in Rome collected provisions for the travelers. Though they were struggling financially themselves they gave willingly. Tychicus found a ship sailing to the coast of Asia. Onesimus volunteered to work as a galley slave to pay for the passage of the two men. He was assured he would be released from service on the ship when they reached Ephesus.

The rowing was harder than it had been before. Onesimus' service to Paul and the brothers had been easy and he was also a few years removed from work on a ship. Still, the knowledge that he was a free man inside helped him deal with the demands of rowing. After he got used to the rhythm of the rowing it became easier. He felt at peace with his situation. Onesimus had made his peace with God. No matter what Philemon decided, Onesimus could face the consequences of his past. He now had communion with God the Father, and did not feel he was facing the future alone. He was serving Christ by serving others. Although he did not know why, God had chosen to find and rescue him from the course he had been on. Being a slave had a purpose now. By serving Philemon he would be serving Jesus Christ.

The trip was favorable. There were some windy days when the rowing was harder, but there were no storms. After passing through the Aegean Sea, they reached the port at Ephesus. Tychicus' first duty was to deliver the letter from Paul to the Church at Ephesus. He read it aloud to the believers there. The letter expressed the plan of God to reconcile to himself all who would believe. He had made all believers a new creation and through Christ, had given each a new nature. The letter went on to explain how men should live because of this new birth. It explained how to relate to each other as well as non-believers. Then he went on to explain how the believer's household should operate. This included the responsibility of those who were slaves.

The letter said: "Slaves, obey your earthly masters with respect and fear, and with sincerity of heart, just as you would obey Christ. Obey them not only to win their favor when their eye is on you, but as slaves of Christ, doing the will of God from your heart. Serve wholeheartedly, as if you are serving the Lord, not people, because you know the Lord will reward each one for whatever good they do, weather they are slave or free."

"And masters, treat your slaves in the same way. Do not threaten them, since you know that he who is both their Master and yours is in heaven, and there is no favoritism with him."[7]

Although this teaching was hard to hear, Onesimus knew it was right. Philemon had purchased him from prison, and he owed his life to Philemon. He only hoped he would still be treated fairly by Philemon. At the cross they were equal.

After reading the letter, Tychicus answered questions about Paul's journey to Rome and why he was there.

"Paul was threatened with death by Jewish leaders in every Gentile town he had preached to, including Ephesus," explained Tychicus. "Paul went to speak with the Jewish leaders in Jerusalem. They rejected

---

[7] *Ephesians 6:5-9f*

his message and again tried to silence him by putting him in prison for treason. Paul had done nothing to deserve these charges, so he was compelled to appeal to Caesar to defend his right to speak. He is renting a house in Rome while his case is decided."

"Will we ever speak with Paul again," asked one believer. "Will he ever be free to leave Rome?"

"I know it is Paul's desire to visit here," said Tychicus. "If he can't come, he will send Timothy to you. When I return to Rome, I will tell Paul of your faithfulness."

The believers gathered to celebrate the Lord's supper. Onesimus served bread and wine. When everyone had been served, they all participated together. Then Onesimus and Tychicus left the house and started on the road to Colossae.

"You served well today, Onesimus," said Tychicus after they had reached the gate of the city of Ephesus. "Is there anything you wish to know now."

"What will happen to me if Philemon does not receive me?" asked Onesimus. "Do I return to Rome with you, or will I be sent to prison?"

"I believe Philemon will receive you," said Tychicus. "I trust the instructions of Paul will be carried out. If he does reject you, I will offer to pay whatever he requests to keep you out of prison."

"I have come to love serving bread and wine to the believers," stated Onesimus. "I hope Philemon will allow me to serve in the house."

"Have faith in God's plan for you," said Tychicus. "You are now a child of God, bought by the blood of Christ. If your desire is to serve others as you have been doing, I am sure God will grant your request."

It was a two-day journey to Colossae, Onesimus had time to think about what he had done to Philemon and his household. He had betrayed

Philemon's trust. He had stolen money from his master. Onesimus was preparing himself for work as a farm laborer. That is what he deserved, even with the appeal from Paul. He did not know if he was able to work in the vineyard. He had grown soft waiting on tables. He had no right to displace the servants who had taken his place.

Tychicus advised Onesimus to stay overnight with the believers from Ephesus who were traveling with them, while he went on ahead to deliver the letter to Philemon. Tychicus would come back to them when he spoke to Philemon and knew what he would do. The believers who came from Ephesus were slaves also, sent by their master to present gifts to the believers in Colossae. The two men rejoiced at the opportunity to serve Christ directly by going on this journey with Tychicus and Onesimus. When they had come to believe in the Christ they saw their need for a savior. The men had surrendered their own resentment at life's unfairness. And they were touched by the sacrifice of Christ. They understood the humility of Jesus Christ in coming to earth not as a King but as a servant. They had experienced the mercy of God. They were slaves together for the same master and in God's mercy they had been introduced to the one true God. Their testimony before Onesimus had encouraged him greatly. Because their master was a believer, they were not afraid of punishment or abuse. And now with Paul's letter, they saw their works as being unto Christ. The two men shared their thoughts with Onesimus. They discussed their lives late into the night.

The next morning, Tychicus returned to the camp. Onesimus was anxious to hear what Philemon had said.

"Philemon is not the same man as when you left him," said Tychicus. "He is suspicious of his house servants and even tried to sell his wine himself, traveling alone. He was assaulted by robbers but made it home and recovered physically."

"He blames me for what happened to him," said Onesimus. "I did not mean for anything to happen to him."

"I know you didn't," said Tychicus. "Deep down I think Philemon knows that too. He told me to take you to his house for the reading of Paul's letter to the church. He promised no harm would come to you. You will have to sit during the passing of the bread and wine."

"I understand why he is not ready to reinstate me," said Onesimus. "I will miss serving the Lord's Supper."

"You are welcome to the service for the reading of Paul's letter," said Tychicus. "Remember, Philemon is a man of peace, just trying to make a living in the best way possible."

"Yes, he is an honest man and a believer," said Onesimus. "I hope he can trust me to serve him for the rest of my life."

"I am relieved to hear you say that" said Tychicus. "He needs someone he can trust. He is not well. The two servants in his house now do their best but are better suited to laboring in the vineyard. They have come to know Philemon well and have been overseers as well as house servants."

Onesimus thought about the way he had served Paul and his companions. He felt useful and fulfilled. There was joy in serving as part of Paul's ministry. He believed that he could find joy in serving in the house church in Colossae. Each meeting he could prepare the bread and wine for the Lord's supper.

Sunday evening the church came to hear the letter Paul had written to the church at Colossae. Philemon was seated at a table near the front. Apphia and Archippus sat with him. Onesimus stood in the back hoping not to be noticed, while Tychicus proceeded to the front of the room. In his letter Paul had stated: For this reason, since the day we heard about you, we have not stopped praying for you. We continually ask God to fill you with the knowledge of his will through all the wisdom and understanding that the Spirit gives, so that you may live a life worthy of the Lord and please him in every way: bearing fruit in every good work, growing in the knowledge of God, being strengthened with all power according to his glorious might so that you may have great endurance and patience, and giving joyful thanks to the Father, who has qualified you to share in the inheritance of his holy people in the kingdom of light.[8]

Philemon was listening to the words of the letter. His heart was stirred. There was more to the life in Christ than escaping judgement. It was about knowing God and living in the power of Christ. We each had a place in the kingdom of God. Philemon knew he could not operate his vineyard without slaves. But he saw the workers as men like himself. His servants all attended the meeting. Philemon had never excluded any of them or made them work on meeting days. But he had been unable to trust the servants in his own house because of what Onesimus had done. Now he was being asked to forgive and welcome him back. Philemon could only do so with the help of the Holy Spirit within him. Onesimus had changed, now Philemon needed to change. When it came time to share the bread and the wine, Philemon knew what he needed to do. He got up and took the bread and broke the loaves and distributed the wine as Archippus recited the ordinance as he had every Sunday for years. When Philemon came to the corner where Onesimus was standing, he stated "the body of Christ broken for you". When he distributed the wine he said, "the blood of Christ, shed for you." When Philemon had finished, he embraced Onesimus and said, "Welcome home brother." And the two men wept.

---

[8]   *Colossians 1: 9-12*

www.ingramcontent.com/pod-product-compliance
Lightning Source LLC
Chambersburg PA
CBHW020346130626
46549CB00003B/1317